About Skill Builders
Cursive
Handwriting
Grades 3+

Skill Builders *Cursive Handwriting* was developed to provide parents and teachers with a tool for reinforcing handwriting skills as children progress from printing into cursive.

This book begins with instruction pages for making each of the letters in the contemporary cursive style. These include a tracing exercise to give students the chance to shape each letter in its uppercase and lowercase form, followed by space they can use to practice writing the letter on their own. From there, the book moves on to word and sentence formation. There is a practice page for each letter with words that begin with that letter, followed by a practice page for each letter with words that begin with that letter in a sentence.

carsondellosa.com
Carson-Dellosa Publishing LLC
Greensboro, North Carolina

Printed in the USA • All rights reserved.

ISBN: 978-1-936023-16-5
10-095161151

Table of Contents

Trace and write each letter.

Alphabet: Letters A–Z

Trace and write each letter.

C c c c

C C C

C c c c

C C C

d d d

D D D

d d d

D D D

Alphabet: Letters A–Z

© Carson-Dellosa

Trace and write each letter.

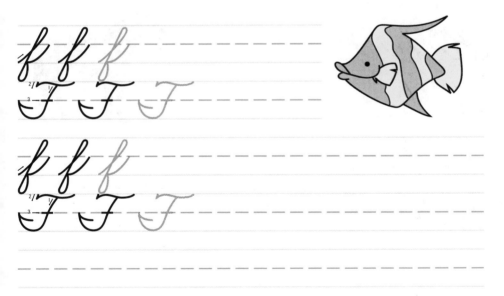

Trace and write each letter.

g g g
G G G

g g g
G G G

h h h
H H H

h h h
H H H

Trace and write each letter.

Trace and write each letter.

Alphabet: Letters A–Z

© Carson-Dellosa

Trace and write each letter.

m m m

m m m

m m m

m m m

m m m

n n n

m m m

n n n

Trace and write each letter.

Alphabet: Letters A–Z

© Carson-Dellosa

Trace and write each letter.

q q q
Q Q Q

q q q
Q Q Q

r r r
R R R

r r r
R R R

Alphabet: Letters A–Z

Trace and write each letter.

$s\ s\ s$

$S\ S\ S$

$s\ s\ s$

$S\ S\ S$

$t\ t\ t$

$T\ T\ T$

$t\ t\ t$

$T\ T\ T$

Alphabet: Letters A–Z

© Carson-Dellosa

Trace and write each letter.

uu uu uu

U U U

uu uu uu

U U U

v v v

V V V

v v v

V V V

Alphabet: Letters A–Z

Trace and write each letter.

w w w

W W W

w w w

W W W

x x x

X X X

x x x

X X X

Trace and write each letter.

Alphabet: Letters A–Z

Trace and write the letter and the words. Then, write a silly sentence using some words from the page.

A A

a a

Ava Ava

ant ant

an an

am am

are are

ate ate

air air

Alphabet: Words and Sentences A–Z   © Carson-Dellosa

Trace and write the sentence.

Alvin the alligator ate an apple.

Alvin the alligator ate an apple.

Alphabet: Words and Sentences A–Z

Trace and write the letter and the words. Then, write a silly sentence using some words from the page.

B B

b b

Blaine Blaine

bus bus

big big

bat bat

bed bed

bird bird

bear bear

Alphabet: Words and Sentences A–Z

© Carson-Dellosa

Trace and write the sentence.

Benji Bear
bounces the beach
ball.

Benji Bear
bounces the beach
ball.

Trace and write the letter and the words. Then, write a silly sentence using some words from the page.

C C

c c

Carlos Carlos

car car

cat cat

cow cow

can can

cup cup

calf calf

Trace and write the sentence.

Chloe Cow watches
Craig crab crawl.

Chloe Cow watches
Craig crab crawl.

Alphabet: Words and Sentences A–Z

Trace and write the letter and the words. Then, write a silly sentence using some words from the page.

$\mathcal{D}$ $\mathcal{D}$

d d

$\mathcal{D}ante$ $\mathcal{D}ante$

day day

did did

do do

dry dry

dog dog

duck duck

Trace and write the sentence.

Dawn Dolphin dives down deep.

Dawn Dolphin dives down deep.

Alphabet: Words and Sentences A–Z 23

Trace and write the letter and the words. Then, write a silly sentence using some words from the page.

$\mathcal{E}$ $\mathcal{E}$

e e

Emma Emma

eat eat

each each

eye eye

ear ear

even even

eel eel

Trace and write the sentence.

Edgar Elephant sits on an egg.

Edgar Elephant sits on an egg.

Trace and write the letter and the words. Then, write a silly sentence using some words from the page.

F F

f f

Felipe Felipe

fan fan

frog frog

for for

fig fig

fox fox

fish fish

Trace and write the sentence.

Find five funny friendly fish.

Find five funny friendly fish.

Trace and write the letter and the words. Then, write a silly sentence using some words from the page.

G G

g g

Greg Greg

gas gas

gym gym

get get

go go

guitar guitar

give give

Trace and write the sentence.

Grace the giraffe gazes at giant gumballs.

Grace the giraffe gazes at giant gumballs.

Trace and write the letter and the words. Then, write a silly sentence using some words from the page.

$\mathcal{H}$ $\mathcal{H}$

h h

Hunter Hunter

hen hen

horse horse

harp harp

hit hit

hay hay

hat hat

Alphabet: Words and Sentences A–Z

© Carson-Dellosa

Trace and write the sentence.

Is Hector Horse hiding in the hay?

Is Hector Horse hiding in the hay?

Trace and write the letter and the words. Then, write a silly sentence using some words from the page.

I I

i i

Isabel Isabel

it it

if if

in in

itch itch

ivy ivy

ice ice

Alphabet: Words and Sentences A–Z   © Carson-Dellosa

Trace and write the sentence.

Ian Iguana eats icky insects.

Ian Iguana eats icky insects.

Trace and write the letter and the words. Then, write a silly sentence using some words from the page.

Jelly

J J

j j

Jasper Jasper

jar jar

job job

jelly jelly

jail jail

jug jug

jet jet

Trace and write the sentence.

Jackie the jaguar jumps with jewelry.

Jackie the jaguar jumps with jewelry.

Trace and write the letter and the words. Then, write a silly sentence using some words from the page.

K K
k k
Kayla Kayla
kid kid
keep keep
key key
knit knit
keg keg
king king

Alphabet: Words and Sentences A–Z   © Carson-Dellosa

Trace and write the sentence.

Katie Kangaroo flies a kite.

Katie Kangaroo flies a kite.

Trace and write the letter and the words. Then, write a silly sentence using some words from the page.

L L

l l

Lin Lin

leg leg

let let

lid lid

log log

lips lips

lion lion

© Carson-Dellosa

Trace and write the sentence.

Lamar the llama laughs at Liza Lizard's joke.

Lamar the llama laughs at Liza Lizard's joke.

Trace and write the letter and the words. Then, write a silly sentence using some words from the page.

M M

m m

Myong Myong

mad mad

men men

mug mug

mix mix

mop mop

mill mill

Alphabet: Words and Sentences A–Z

© Carson-Dellosa

Trace and write the sentence.

Myra Mouse dances to music.

Myra Mouse dances to music.

Trace and write the letter and the words. Then, write a silly sentence using some words from the page.

n n

n n

Nathan Nathan

nut nut

nap nap

not not

nine nine

net net

nest nest

Trace and write the sentence.

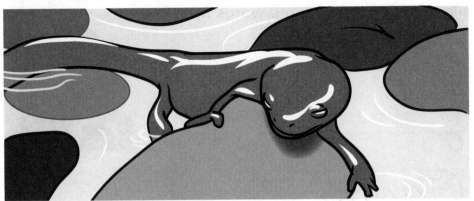

Nora the newt
naps at moon.
Nora the newt
naps at moon.

Trace and write the letter and the words. Then, write a silly sentence using some words from the page.

O O

o o

Owen Owen

old old

out out

one one

ox ox

oil oil

owl owl

Trace and write the sentence.

Olivia Ostrich
likes to watch
Orlando Octopus.

Olivia Ostrich
likes to watch
Orlando Octopus.

Trace and write the letter and the words. Then, write a silly sentence using some words from the page.

P P

p p

Paige Paige

put put

pan pan

pen pen

pop pop

play play

pin pin

Alphabet: Words and Sentences A–Z

© Carson-Dellosa

Trace and write the sentence.

Penny the penguin plays with a pumpkin.

Penny the penguin plays with a pumpkin.

Trace and write the letter and the words. Then, write a silly sentence using some words from the page.

Q Q

q q

Quinn Quinn

quail quail

quick quick

quiet quiet

quit quit

quest quest

queen queen

Trace and write the sentence.

Quiet Quan
the quail quilts
quickly.

Quiet Quan
the quail quilts
quickly.

Alphabet: Words and Sentences A–Z

Trace and write the letter and the words. Then, write a silly sentence using some words from the page.

R R

r r

Rashad Rashad

red red

ran ran

rug rug

rock rock

ride ride

rabbit rabbit

Alphabet: Words and Sentences A–Z
© Carson-Dellosa

Trace and write the sentence.

Ryan Rooster and
Ramsey the rat
run in the rain.

Ryan Rooster and
Ramsey the rat
run in the rain.

Trace and write the letter and the words. Then, write a silly sentence using some words from the page.

$\mathcal{S}$ $\mathcal{S}$

s s

Sam Sam

sad sad

sky sky

she she

sun sun

sit sit

snail snail

Alphabet: Words and Sentences A–Z · © Carson-Dellosa

Trace and write the sentence.

Samia Snake
tells Scott the
skunk a secret.

Samia Snake
tells Scott the
skunk a secret.

Alphabet: Words and Sentences A–Z

Trace and write the letter and the words. Then, write a silly sentence using some words from the page.

$\mathcal{T}\,\mathcal{T}$

$t\ t$

Tyrone Tyrone

tag tag

tell tell

tree tree

two two

tub tub

turtle turtle

Alphabet: Words and Sentences A–Z

© Carson-Dellosa

Trace and write the sentence.

Timothy Tiger took a trip to Texas.

Timothy Tiger took a trip to Texas.

Trace and write the letter and the words. Then, write a silly sentence using some words from the page.

$\mathcal{U}$ $\mathcal{U}$

u u

$\mathcal{U}ma$ $\mathcal{U}ma$

use use

up up

$uncle$ $uncle$

$ultra$ $ultra$

$under$ $under$

$unicorn$ $unicorn$

Alphabet: Words and Sentences A–Z   © Carson-Dellosa

Trace and write the sentence.

Ursula Unicorn
is not under the
umbrella.

Ursula Unicorn
is not under the
umbrella.

Alphabet: Words and Sentences A–Z

Trace and write the letter and the words. Then, write a silly sentence using some words from the page.

$\mathcal{V}$ $\mathcal{V}$

v v

Vanessa *Vanessa*

very *very*

voice *voice*

van *van*

view *view*

vase *vase*

vacuum *vacuum*

Trace and write the sentence.

Victor Vulture
received a
valentine.

Victor Vulture
received a
valentine.

Alphabet: Words and Sentences A–Z

Trace and write the letter and the words. Then, write a silly sentence using some words from the page.

$\mathcal{W}\,\mathcal{W}$

$w\ w$

Wesley Wesley

will will

wag wag

web web

wasp wasp

wax wax

wolf wolf

Alphabet: Words and Sentences A–Z

© Carson-Dellosa

Trace and write the sentence.

Wallace the walrus was in waves.

Wallace the walrus was in waves.

Trace and write the letter and the words. Then, write a silly sentence using some words from the page.

$\mathcal{X}$ $\mathcal{X}$

x x

Xavier *Xavier*

X-ray *X-ray*

box *box*

axe *axe*

exit *exit*

mix *mix*

xerox *xerox*

Alphabet: Words and Sentences A–Z

© Carson-Dellosa

Trace and write the sentence.

Xander the fox looks at a xylophone.

Xander the fox looks at a xylophone.

Trace and write the letter and the words. Then, write a
silly sentence using some words from the page.

$\mathcal{Y}$ $\mathcal{Y}$

y y

Yvette Yvette

yell yell

yes yes

you you

yet yet

yeah yeah

yarn yarn

© Carson-Dellosa

Trace and write the sentence.

Yuri the yak
plays with yellow
yarn.

Yuri the yak
plays with yellow
yarn.

Trace and write the letter and the words. Then, write a silly sentence using some words from the page.

z z

z z

zeb zeb

zap zap

zig zig

zag zag

zoom zoom

zebra zebra

zipper zipper

Trace and write the sentence.

Joe Zebra likes to do puzzles.

Joe Zebra likes to do puzzles.

Trace and write each number.

1 1

one one

one balloon

2 2

two two

two balloons

3 3

three three

three balloons

Trace and write each number.

4 4

four four

four balloons

5 5

five five

five balloons

6 6

six six

six balloons

Trace and write each number.

7 7

seven *seven*

seven balloons

8 8

eight *eight*

eight balloons

9 9

nine *nine*

nine balloons

© Carson-Dellosa

Trace and write each number.

$10 \quad 10$ --- --- --- ---

ten ten --- --- ---

--- --- --- --- --- --- --- --- ---

ten balloons

$11 \quad 11$ --- --- --- ---

eleven --- --- ---

eleven --- --- --- ---

eleven balloons

$12 \quad 12$ --- --- --- ---

twelve --- --- ---

twelve --- --- --- ---

twelve balloons

Write the name of each color.

red

yellow

blue

green

black

brown

orange

purple

Write the name of each shape.

pentagon

oval

hexagon

circle

square

triangle

rhombus

rectangle

Write the name of each food.

pizza

soup

beans

milk

eggs

apple

toast

burrito

Write the name of each food.

corn

juice

yogurt

bread

cereal

melon

cheese

nuts

pear

Write the name of each month.

January

February

March

April

May

June

July

Write the name of each month.

August

September

October

November

December

Write the name of each day.

Monday

Tuesday

Wednesday

Thursday

Friday

Write each word.

Saturday

Sunday

week

month

year

holiday

Write the name of each time.

night -

day -

minute - - - - - - - - - - - - - - - - -

hour - - - - - - - - - - - - - - - - - -

noon - - - - - - - - - - - - - - - - - -

morning - - - - - - - - - - - - -

afternoon - - - - - - - -

- -

evening - - - - - - - - - - - - -

- -

- -